A Long Day at the River

Written by Kerrie Shanahan

Flying Start
to Literacy®

T0342928

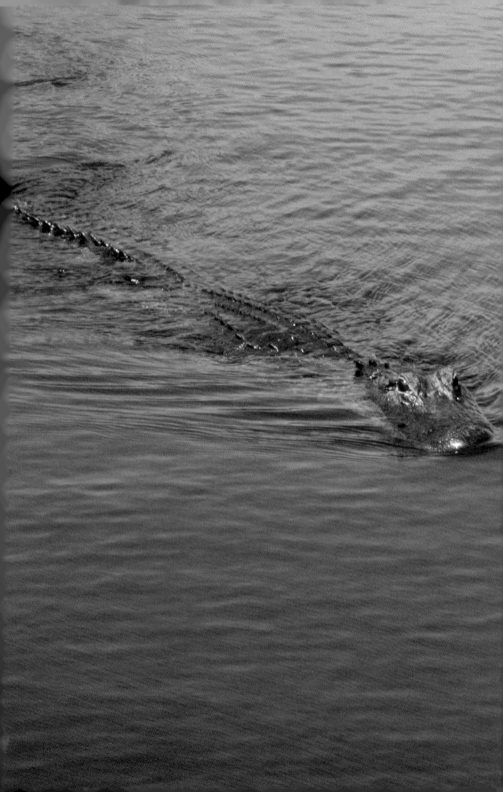

Contents

Morning

Warming up

It is morning down at the river. A large female crocodile lies on the banks of the river in the sun. The sun begins to heat the land.

The crocodile needs the sun's heat.
Like all reptiles, she is cold–blooded.
This means her body temperature is
the same as the temperature around her.

Without the sun's warmth, the crocodile
can only move slowly.

Protecting the nest

The crocodile lies very still, but she is watching for signs of danger. She is protecting her nest, which has more than 50 eggs.

Three months ago, the crocodile used her sharp claws and strong legs to dig a nest in the sand. Then she laid her eggs and scooped the sand back over them.

She has been guarding the eggs ever since. Soon, the eggs will hatch.

Midday
Keeping watch from the river

By midday, the sun is very hot.
The crocodile goes into the river to cool
her body. She is watching for signs
of danger. She is watching for any
animal that might want to eat her
eggs and the baby crocodiles inside.

The crocodile is difficult to see in the
water. The only parts above the water
are her eyes, ears and nostrils. Her
scaly skin blends in with the colour
of the water.

A predator moves in

Suddenly, the crocodile sees something move in the bushes on the riverbank. It is a lizard. It is sniffing around her nest.

The crocodile moves fast. She jumps out of the water. Her strong tail pushes her quickly up the riverbank. Her large jaws are open, showing rows of sharp teeth.

The lizard runs off into the bush. The eggs are still safe.

Evening
The sun sets

As the sun slowly sets, the temperature at the river begins to cool. It is very quiet.

Then a high-pitched sound comes from the crocodile's nest.

Peep! Peep! Peep!

The baby crocodiles are beginning to hatch. The mother crocodile can hear the baby crocodiles. They need her.

Carefully, she digs away the sand covering the eggs so that her babies can hatch.

The eggs hatch

Inside the eggs, the young crocs are chipping away at the shell. They have a tough piece of skin on their nose called an egg tooth. They use the egg tooth to break the egg shell.

The mother crocodile uses her teeth to help her babies hatch out of their eggs. She gently pulls away the shell so her babies can get out.

But, even with their mother's help, only about a quarter of the eggs in the nest hatch.

To the river

The baby crocodiles look like their mother, but they are tiny. They have to get to the water to survive.

The mother crocodile helps some of her babies reach the water by carrying them gently in her mouth.

When they get to the water, the young crocodiles can already swim. They begin to catch insects.

The baby crocodiles stay with their mother for several weeks so that she can protect them from predators.

Only about one in every 50 baby crocodiles will survive to become an adult.

Night
Time to hunt

It is night at the river. The mother crocodile did not eat while she was guarding her nest. She is very hungry.

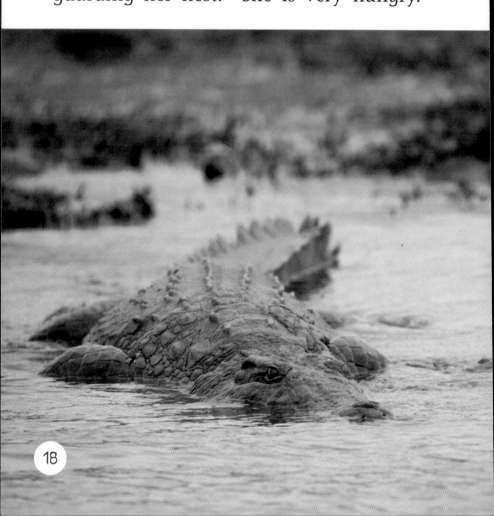

The mother crocodile goes into the river to hunt. She must leave her babies for a short time to hunt an animal to eat.

Crocodiles hunt fish, turtles, birds, buffaloes, monkeys and smaller crocodiles.

Searching for prey

Like all crocodiles, this female crocodile
is a good hunter.

As she swims along, she uses her senses to
search for prey. She has excellent hearing,
smell and sight.

20

She also has special senses in her skin that can detect movement in the water around her.

She uses her strong tail and webbed back feet to move quickly through the water.

Snap!

In the dim light, the crocodile sees a large fish in the river. In one swift move, she snaps the fish in her strong jaws.

The crocodile returns to her young.

All is quiet.

All is calm.

Another day at the river is over.

Index